A Bulldozer's Day

by Harriet Loy
Illustrated by Mike Byrne

BLASTOFF!
MISSIONS

BELLWETHER MEDIA
MINNEAPOLIS, MN

Blastoff! Missions takes you on a learning adventure! Colorful illustrations and exciting narratives highlight cool facts about our world and beyond. Read the mission goals and follow the narrative to gain knowledge, build reading skills, and have fun!

Traditional Nonfiction

Narrative Nonfiction

Blastoff! Universe

MISSION GOALS

⬛ ⬛ ⬛ ⬛ ⬛ ⬛

> FIND YOUR SIGHT WORDS IN THE BOOK.

> LEARN ABOUT THE DIFFERENT JOBS A BULLDOZER HAS.

> BE ABLE TO IDENTIFY THREE DIFFERENT PARTS OF A BULLDOZER.

This edition first published in 2023 by Bellwether Media, Inc.

No part of this publication may be reproduced in whole or in part without written permission of the publisher. For information regarding permission, write to Bellwether Media, Inc., Attention: Permissions Department, 6012 Blue Circle Drive, Minnetonka, MN 55343.

Library of Congress Cataloging-in-Publication Data

LC record for A Bulldozer's Day available at: https://lccn.loc.gov/2022013620

Text copyright © 2023 by Bellwether Media, Inc. BLASTOFF! MISSIONS and associated logos are trademarks and/or registered trademarks of Bellwether Media, Inc.

Editor: Christina Leaf   Designer: Andrea Schneider

Printed in the United States of America, North Mankato, MN.

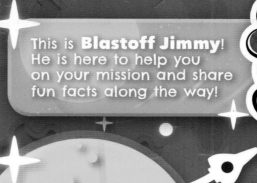

This is **Blastoff Jimmy**! He is here to help you on your mission and share fun facts along the way!

Table of Contents

The Construction Site

excavator

dump truck

The **construction site** is busy! Cranes lift, **excavators** dig, and dump trucks **haul**.

But one machine stands out from the rest. It is the mighty bulldozer!

bulldozer

construction site

5

An **operator** climbs into the bulldozer's **cab**. He starts the **engine**.

The engine rumbles, and the **tracks** start to move. Time to work!

JIMMY SAYS

A bulldozer's tracks help it move across rough, rocky ground. They also keep the bulldozer from sinking into softer ground.

cab

operator

tracks

7

Rocks in the Way

The bulldozer has many jobs to do today. First, it must move a big pile of rocks. The rocks weigh hundreds of pounds!

They are no match for the bulldozer's power and strong **blade**.

blade

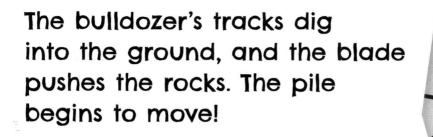

The bulldozer's tracks dig
into the ground, and the blade
pushes the rocks. The pile
begins to move!

Soon, the job is done.
The rocks will be loaded into
a dump truck and taken away.

Next, the bulldozer needs to rip up some rough and rocky ground. The operator prepares the **ripper** on the back of the machine.

The ripper digs into the ground. The bulldozer crawls forward.

ripper

The ripper cuts through
the tough ground.
It breaks up big rocks
and chunks of dirt.

The bulldozer keeps going.
Soon, the ground is all
ripped up.

What a mess. The bulldozer can clean it up!

Its big blade pushes the dirt and rocks out of the way. The bulldozer is strong!

JIMMY SAYS

The first bulldozer was made in 1923. It was used to bury a pipeline.

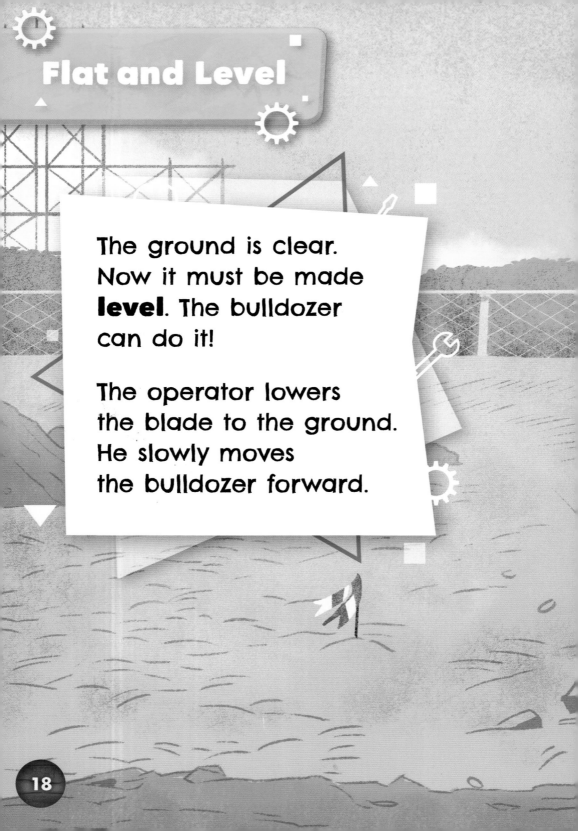

Flat and Level

The ground is clear.
Now it must be made
level. The bulldozer
can do it!

The operator lowers
the blade to the ground.
He slowly moves
the bulldozer forward.

The bulldozer moves back
and forth many times.
Soon, the ground is flat.
It is ready for a building.
Great work, bulldozer!

Bulldozer Jobs

move rocks

level ground

rip up hard ground

Glossary

blade–the flat part at the front of a bulldozer that pushes rocks and dirt

cab–the place where the driver sits

construction site–a place where building projects are done

engine–the part of a bulldozer that makes it go

excavators–machines that dig

haul–to carry

level–flat

operator–a person who works a machine

ripper–a sharp part on the back of a bulldozer that tears up ground

tracks–loops around wheels on a bulldozer to help it move

To Learn More

AT THE LIBRARY

Arnold, Quinn M. *Bulldozers*. Mankato, Minn.: Creative Education, 2018.

Carr, Aaron. *Bulldozers*. New York, N.Y.: AV2 by Weigl, 2020.

Murray, Julie. *Bulldozers*. Minneapolis, Minn.: Abdo Zoom, 2019.

ON THE WEB

FACTSURFER

Factsurfer.com gives you a safe, fun way to find more information.

1. Go to www.factsurfer.com.

2. Enter "bulldozers" into the search box and click 🔍.

3. Select your book cover to see a list of related content.

23

BEYOND THE MISSION

> WHAT FACT FROM THE BOOK DID YOU THINK WAS MOST INTERESTING?

> WOULD YOU LIKE TO DRIVE A BULLDOZER? WHY OR WHY NOT?

> DRAW A PICTURE OF A BUILDING THAT YOU WOULD BUILD AT THE BULLDOZER'S CONSTRUCTION SITE.

Index